Hop, Run, and Jump!

by B. G. Hennessy
illustrated by Valeria Petrone

Scott Foresman

Editorial Offices: Glenview, Illinois • New York, New York
Sales Offices: Reading, Massachusetts • Duluth, Georgia
Glenview, Illinois • Carrollton, Texas • Menlo Park, California

Pat came out to play.
She knows how to hop.

Tom came out to play.
He knows how to run fast.

Jill came out to play.
She knows how to jump

Ken came out to play.

He wants to play ball.

He asks them all!

Yes, they all want to play!